How to N

The best negotiation book on training essentials, skills, techniques & style:

Yes, become a business negotiation genius via this in-depth book on the art

of negotiation

Neil Hoechlin

No part of this book may be reproduced or transmitted in any form whatsoever, electronic, or mechanical, including photocopying, recording, or by any informational storage or retrieval system without express permission from the author

Copyright © 2018 JNR Publishing Group

All rights reserved

Introduction	6
Characteristics of negotiation:	6
Prepare yourself for Negotiation	7
Tools for successful negotiation	9
Building your negotiation process	12
Set goals & limits	13
Be a good listener	13
Be clear	14
Communication a key skill of a good negotiator	14
Stay calm while conducting the meeting	14
Push the pause button	14
Closing the deal	15
Putting your ideas into action	15
Handling all types of Negotiations	16
Effective ways to improve your negotiation skills	16
Elements of successful negotiating skills	17
International Negotiations	18
Negotiations among Men & Women	19
Negotiation over the phone and the internet	19
Elements influencing the negotiation process	19
Setting your goals and planning to achieve them	21
Envisioning your future	22
Making a commitment	24
Identifying your values	24
Planning ways to achieve your vision	24
The 3 year plan	25
Maximizing gains must be your main aim behind the negotiations	25
Dressing for success	26
Mapping the opposition	27
Gathering information	28
Setting a good goal	29

Setting the opening offer	29
Setting & enforcing limits	30
Components for a successful business negotiation	30
How to convey your message to the other person when you have decided to walk away	31
The role of listening in the negotiation process	31
Strategies to succeed with difficult customers during negotiation	32
Asking the right questions	33
Battling the Jargon	33
Guidelines to ask quality questions	34
Role of body language while listening	35
Tune in with your inner voice	36
Being crystal clear by expressing your views	36
Organizing your thoughts	36
Keep your commitments	37
Write it down	38
Encouraging others to clarify	38
Capturing the audience	39
Barriers to clarity	39
Turn off the anger buttons by pushing the pause buttons	40
Human beings are full of emotions & responses	41
Your attitude plays a big role during a negotiation	41
Dealing with discouragement	42
Dealing with difficult situations and people	43
Things that can help you enhance your negotiation outcomes	44
Closing the deal- The glory moment	45
Assessing the deal	46
Win-win deals	48
Psychological barriers to closing	48

Introduction

Negotiation is a part of everyone's personal and professional lives.

Every relationship, whether it's a boss or employees, vendors or clients, spouse or kids require constant negotiation.

In simple words, negotiation is any kind of communication which a person strives to achieve by the action, acquiescence or approval of someone else.

Negotiation is not just a skill but a way to get things done in life.

Negotiation (big or small) requires 6 basic skills.

Information sharing (hitting the right persuasion buttons while conveying information), ranking the priorities, knowing when and how to push the pause button, good listening skills, clarity of communication & knowhow or skills on how to close the deal.

Characteristics of negotiation:

Negotiation is a process that involves communication and persuasion between two or more individuals, parties or groups having diverse interests to achieve the desired goals.

The negotiation process starts with the differences between the objectives or opinions of 2 parties which prevents agreement.

The parties involved in negotiation willfully communicate or cooperate to meet their objectives.

The parties involved during negotiation, try to find a mutually beneficial position, by trying their best to influence each other. Both the parties believe that negotiation would produce the desired, or at least acceptable outcomes for all parties concerned. Hence, negotiation is the involvement of two individuals, groups or parties over an agreeable decision for certain issues.

There is always room for improvement for bad communicators during the negotiating process.

Being the negotiator, it is your duty to handle such people to create a better understanding and find mutual agreements.

Creating a better understanding, further helps in understanding and meeting people's needs and wants. However, such people often feel humiliated when you tell them that they are bad at communication, negotiation or difficult to deal with.

When someone lacks the necessary skills, your duty is to pull that person and encourage him to learn better communication and negotiation methods. You have to be tactful while doing this, because the person will open up only when he/ she feels comfortable, and not antagonized. Your approach to tackling that person depends upon the type of person and personality you are dealing with.

Note: During the process of negotiation, you must not feel shy while asking questions from your counterparts. Whenever you feel the need to clarify anything, go ahead to put an end to your curiosity. This is because words hold different meanings when used in various contexts. Even if they mean the same, it is important to clarify when in doubt. Such are called relative words. So clarifying relativity is an important part during the process of negotiation.

In other words, you may say that relative words are descriptive and non-specific words that hold meaning only in relation to something else. Some of these words are substantial, soon, many large, high quality, cheap etc. Never be shy to ask for clarification when such words are used.

Prepare yourself for Negotiation

Whether it's a personal or a professional negotiation, you must be prepared to get your specified goals.

Preparation involves 3 areas which include; the negotiator (you), the other person (with whom you are negotiating) and the environment/setting.

Therefore, before negotiating, you must be clear about what you want, which will help in boosting your confidence and performance. At the same time, you must also know your strengths & weaknesses. For example, do you have the patience to listen to what the other person is saying or you just interrupt in between ignoring what the other person has to convey? Keeping these in mind, you must equip yourself for the negotiation.

It is also important to have some knowledge about the other person before negotiating which can help you gain confidence and maneuver the negotiation in your favor.

For instance, if you are appearing for an interview you must do some research about your interviewer (if possible, or at least the company) which can help you to create better rapport, and give better and more targeted answers-- which in turn increases your chances to get the job.

You must also prepare yourself about the current market conditions or the arena. If a situation demands you to negotiate in a world which is not familiar to you? You must research it beforehand. Study and try to become the smartest person in the room.

Knowledge is power too, and that becomes handy in the course of the negotiation.

Different negotiation styles

- Competitive style
- Co-operative style
- Problem-solving style

Tools for successful negotiation

The process of negotiation is supported by various tools from the negotiation toolbox. Using the right tool at the right time helps you in availing of the benefits of the situation.

At the same time, it helps you hold command over the negotiation process.

Some of these tools are as follows:

Trust-- This tool or principle must be taken into account with great importance. No negotiation can take place on this earth in the absence of the "trust" factor. During the negotiation process, it is assumed that the parties or individuals involved in the negotiation process trust and respect each other.

Perception- Perception is the alignment of your image-- that you are trying to project in front of others along with the attitude that you are carrying.

This is because the person in front of you is going to learn more from you by looking at your attitude irrespective of what you are saying.

If you are weak in conveying at what you believe, then people might not believe you.

Strategies & tactics- Using the predetermined strategies and tactics at the right time during negotiation helps in your chances of success. Provided you use the right strategies & tactics.

There are stages involved in the process of negotiation

Stage 1- Assess and choose the strategy that helps to solve problems or get what you want.

This can be done by assessing your options, leverage and various procedures and approaches in court, arbitration, mediation, facilitation, negotiation.

Once you have selected an approach, move on to the next stage.

Stage 2- Communicate with the other party or parties.

This can be done via mail, phone or in person.

Make them understand the reason behind your deal in terms of your desires & coordinate approaches.

Expand relationship by building rapport and establishing your value and your proposals, likewise building your organization's & personal credibility.

Stage 3- Analyze background information.

This involves collecting relevant facts and figures about the other party.

Verify the information before moving ahead.

Identify psychological, procedural and substantive interests of all the people involved.

Stage 4- Design an effective negotiation plan.

It involves different types of tactics and strategies that encourage them to consider the deal.

It also involves ways to deal with various situations and problem areas at the time of negotiation.

Stage 5- This stage consists of building trust & cooperation that lays the foundation for every deal.

A negotiator must have proper strategies to tackle strong emotions mainly anger and resentment.

It also involves legitimate recognition and addressing of problems and personal issues of the people involved.

Here, clarity communication in plays an important role.

Stage 6- Initiating a negotiation session.

It involves the introduction of the parties involved, establishing ground rules such as behavioral guidelines, identifying interests, mutual expectations, idea sharing, willingness to listen, openness and desire to negotiate in a good faith.

Stage 7- Set an agenda by defining issues.

It involves identifying areas of concern, problem solving of the interests of all the parties involved.

Gain additional information via proper listening, asking open ended questions and discussing issues.

Stage 8- Reveal hidden interests.

It involves identifying interests of people at the time of the dispute.

This is done so that everyone understands the interest of each other and tries to agrees on a common point.

Stage 9- Generating alternatives to arrive at amicable agreements.

The issues or the needs of the parties are reviewed.

Creating awareness, generating objective standards, brainstorming, applying trial and error, generating multiple solutions, looking for win-win solutions and trading concessions which are valued differently by each party.

Stage 10- Assessing alternatives for settlement- Taking into account the alternatives for reaching a settlement.

Calculating the advantages and costs of selecting each option, assessing the interest of the parties involved and finding alternate ways on how those interests can be met.

Stage-11- Here comes the final negotiation phase, which is the most important part of every negotiation.

Establish substantive agreements by offering incremental concessions in order to close the deal.

Stage 12- Achieving formal settlement- It involves the legal contract or a memorandum of agreement (written), monitoring evaluation procedures.

Lastly the development of enforcement & commitments mechanisms takes place here.
Setting your goals require disciplined focus and a lot of preparation.

When you are not alone, you also have to set goals for your team, to avoid confusions between your goals and day dreaming.

For instance, planning to write the bestselling book is day dreaming. But planning to write a book about a particular subject that can make a solid contribution to society is a goal.

Set realistic goals you can achieve from the negotiation.

Building your negotiation process

The process of negotiation must be built considering the following areas in mind.

- Real base
- Aspiration base
- Deal qualification
- Identification of objectives behind the deal (for yourself and the other person)
- Contracting zone
- Clarity in the definition of negotiation & team composition
- Negotiation tactics & deal specific strategies such as framing, scripts, procedures to close the deal etc.

Apart from the above factors, you must also find ways to establish a negotiation-conducive environment. This helps the negotiators participate actively on a daily basis minus unnecessary distractions.

Creating a database for negotiation is also a good idea to conduct a more consistent and professional negotiation. What spiels, tactics, rebuttals etc.

Introducing automation by enhancing the usage of negotiation supporting tools and analytics will also help, such as the CRM and other software used in call centers for example.

Leading or coaching team members with negotiation best practices by higher level managers and trainers who are specially trained to do the same on a regular basis.

This coaching can also be done on an individual basis if required.

Set goals & limits

As already discussed, setting your goals require disciplined focus and a lot of preparation. When you are not alone, you also have to set goals for your team.

Setting limits involve knowing you have other choices too & detailed knowledge about what those choices are.

Enforcing limits involve writing down your limits, establishing your resistance point, imparting knowledge to the entire team and stop painting yourself into a corner.

Setting goals are the only way to achieve success.

Setting goals involve brainstorming sessions and clarifying what you really want, and things you are willing to compromise on.

Try to also explore all the possibilities for any kind of negotiation.

The best way to follow your goals is to write them down so that you can visualize your goals before achieving them.

Be a good listener

Many believe that they are good listeners even when they are not.

Honestly, improve on your listening skills because your listening skills will determine your success while negotiation. Try to improve your listening skills on a regular basis because the rewards are amazing.

Below are few tips to become a good listener:

- First, clear away the mess at your workplace.
- Second, count numbers before answering to questions or comments.

- Third is attentive while the other person is talking to you.

Be clear

You must be confident in what you are saying. It means your speech, body language, actions, tone of voice all convey the same message (congruence).

Communication a key skill of a good negotiator

The best way is to set your purpose or intent while speaking to avoid useless yammering, and be specific, to create a powerful, compelling argument.

Stay calm while conducting the meeting

Learn to deal tactfully.

This can be done by giving constructive contribution to the meeting. Ask questions to seek their views and reactions.

Intervene, pause or break the conversation when necessary.

Restrain the ramblers (from your team) as they dilute the effect of the communication and lead to boredom and general time wasting

Push the pause button

A pause button is necessary to keep emotional distance while negotiating.

Some people use the pause button quite frequently while some don't feel like using it at all.

For instance, a pause button can be used during a heated debate to create silence when both the parties do not agree upon each other's viewpoint.

It also helps to calm down a person and restrict him/ her from saying something that could later be regretted.

While in some situations, the absence of the pause button helps you crack your deal as the other person doesn't get enough time to think about your offer.

Hence, while negotiating, people should not let their emotions control their actions.

So avoid using your hot buttons and start using the pause button.

Closing the deal

Most of the time, the deal still does not get finalized even when both parties agree on the important issues.

There may be various reasons for the same, such as someone being too demanding, someone being a bully or someone is intentionally creating disturbances during proceedings.

To overcome such situations, take breaks wherever required so that people get a chance to regroup.

Sometimes invisible partners also create disturbances.

So while you are on break, try to study your opponent's strategies, so that when you are back on the negotiation table, you can easily deal with these obstructions.

Closing the deal is sometimes not as easy as it seems to be.

This is because sometime you may come across people who may never like your offer no matter how good it is. In such cases, ask more questions to help solve the other person's problem.

Most of the time, the hurdles while closing the deal is not due to you or any other external factors, but the obstacles lie within your inner self. Here you have to fight your own demons and not anyone else. Once you have identified your fears, take steps to eradicate them. Once this is done you would be better equipped to handle objections people place in front of you.

Putting your ideas into action

Take initiatives to achieve your goals.

You need to perform specific tasks as per your plan and make sure that everything goes as smooth as possible as it was conceived.

This will help in making you more effective and efficient.

Creating your action plans require the following:

- Prioritize goals.
- Identifying actions that are required while performing specific goals.
- Identifying important individuals who can assist you in performing each action.
- Identifying obstacles while performing each action.
- Estimating the date of completion of all your action plans.

Handling all types of Negotiations

Irrespective of the situation, you can apply the basic negotiating actions to every negotiation. However, there are some negotiations that are beyond the reach of these skills but, you still have to focus on these basic skills.

Effective ways to improve your negotiation skills

Avoid over compromising while negotiating- Negotiation does not always mean compromising or bending over backwards to the wills of the opposing party.

To get the ideal result, try to make the other person fully understand and do your damn best to convince him to agree to the deal as is, instead of compromising.

Highlight the benefits of your deal as per the person's needs and wants.

Perhaps compromise on moot points that will not affect you too much?

Make the difference- It is possible that other companies are also offering similar products and services in the same price or priced lower than yours.

In such situations, try to make the other person understand how your offer is unique from all of them in best meeting their needs. This should be done with proper research quiet in advance. To do so, you must possess the power to influence and present your case persuasively.

Listening- Listening is one of the most important skills during the entire negotiation process. This is because people do not buy goods from vendors who do not listen carefully to their requirements.

Research has shown that people who are not heard carefully feel unloved, ignored and unimportant.

Listening is accompanied by 3 basic levels- selective listening that involves listening to only those things that you feel are important, responsive listening which involves physical and verbal feedback such as asking or nodding and playback listening which involves restating what you heard to confirm to him that you fully understand and is truly listening to him.

Make proper plans before the negotiation takes place- It involves researching and preparing a written note on what topics you are going to cover during your presentation at the negotiation.

Make a list of possible talking points, the objections and with rebuttals, the spiels etc.

Elements of successful negotiating skills

- You clearly know what you want.
- You clearly know the needs and wants of the other party.
- You are taking into account the method and step by step process of the negotiations, until closing phase is reached.
- Preparing your presentation point by point.
- Offering benefits or value added services and counter-offers in return for acceptance of your deal.
- Preparing alternative offers for mutual gains.

- Ways to deal with complicated negotiations

You can apply the basic negotiating skills but how to handle situations when negotiation keeps becoming complicated?

This complexity arises when the situation demands the involvement of more than 2 people. Hence when the negotiation shifts from 2 people to 30 people it becomes a nightmare!

In other words, you may say that negotiation becomes complicated when a person invests all the effort & emotion to each get what they want.

Salary negotiation is one such example.

International Negotiations

Cross cultural negotiations or international negotiation is a specialized area in the negotiating world.

In such kind of negotiations, the basic skills do not hold much importance because these negotiations require extra preparation.

In such situations the negotiator has to tailor the negotiating approach as per the customs of the country where the negotiation is taking place.

It requires know-how on how the foreigners close a deal in terms of attitude, business etiquette, customs, behavior while handling conflicts, their communication process, decision making procedure, the way of disclosing information and how they finalize a deal.

Every country has its own body language too.

To succeed, you must research the country's traditions before starting the talks. You may learn key phrases, read the travel guide, watch movies while preparing etc. In order to close the deal, you have to behave like a native and respect the customs in that country.

Negotiations among Men & Women

Communication between men and women is much more simplified and progressive now than in the past. This is because women are now players in politics and big businesses. But we cannot deny the fact that fundamental differences still set them apart.

Negotiation over the phone and the internet

Technological advancements have changed the mode people negotiate with each other. The expanding use of internet and telephone has made this possible.

Communication via internet and phone is simpler and faster these days because it allows you to negotiate through the comfort of your office, home, car from any part of the world.

However, negotiations via such means will lack the personal touch in terms of gestures, body language, and human interactions.

In case of face to face interactions, it is extremely important for you to match your body language with your words.

If you fail to do so you must find out the reasons for the same and take appropriate actions right away.

This is because it may make you appear insincere or weak and unconfident.

Elements influencing the negotiation process

There are various elements that influence the smooth functioning of the negotiation process. To make the negotiation successful, it is essential to work over these elements. Some of these factors are the following:

Negotiator- The success of every negotiation entirely depends on the skills and abilities of the negotiator.

The credibility and character of the negotiator play a big role in influencing the parties involved in the process. This is because it is the prime duty of the negotiator to keep control over the entire process.

A person must be capable enough to build a positive attitude towards the deal he is expecting to finalize.

Parties- The way the parties involved in the negotiation process react & respond towards the negotiation process also influences the success of the negotiation.

This is because when mismatching views and ideas, some of them might fail to tackle the situation wisely.

Team selection- The team of negotiators must be selected on the basis of situation and cases.

Each person must be capable enough to contribute towards achieving the pre-determined goals in a productive way.

Venue of negotiation- The place of negotiation must be chosen with utmost care because unfamiliar noises & surroundings may cause stress among those individuals who are not familiar with the same.

Room layout- The room layout must be such that the people who are supposed to sit there must get the same or similar kind of working environment in which they regularly work. In other words, they should feel comfortable.

Also the seating arrangement must be comfortable enough to allow proper communications. Power plays also rely on positioning.

The distance between each person should not be too far.

Psychology in negotiation- Psychology in negotiation relates to the psychological gambits that will be used in various activities at the time of negotiation. Every individual has his own approach, attitude, and perception when conducting different kinds of activities. You need to pinpoint and work with those considerations in mind.

This is directly related to an individual's needs and wants, which are classified as:

- Ego needs,
- Physical & survival needs,
- Self-realization needs,
- Security & safety needs &
- Social needs

Setting your goals and planning to achieve them

If the first step is to set your goals then the next important step is to prepare yourself to achieve them.

You must be clear about the dos and don'ts in your personal and professional life especially in negotiations.

- What are your boundaries?
- How far are you willing to go to get what you want?
- What will you not tolerate from others?
- And so on.

Many people fail to get success and end up blaming their negotiating skills in which probably it is their inner game, or having the wrong values which are preventing them from reaching success.

In this arena, you gotta be ruthless sometimes too.

Using negotiating skills more effectively require building a master plan. This master plan contains strategies to convert your dreams into reality. All it takes is challenging yourself to control the main areas of your life.

Be proactive and not reactive. Creating your vision

Many successful businesses have their vision/ mission statement.

You may see these statements even published over their websites & printed over their publications.

Every employee follows the same mission/vision while working in that company. But personally in their own lives & career they do not have any mission statement. To lead a successful life one must have some agenda about both the long & short term goals. The clearer the goal will be, the smoother the negotiation is likely to happen and vice versa steering towards that direction.

This might seem too big picture or trivial? But this is important especially in sales teams or negotiation teams, because they are the face of the company in the eyes of the other parties in a meeting.

They should conduct themselves in alignment with a particular company's mission/vision objectives.

Some examples of the vision statements of some renowned and successful companies are:

Microsoft- *"Someday we will see a computer on every desk and in every home".*

Young businessman- *"To climb up the corporate ladder in an honest and professional way".*

My law office- *"To help my clients realize their dreams".*

Envisioning your future

Those who write down their mission statements find it easier to convert their dreams into reality. You must sit down alone or with your partner to start thinking about your goals in life.

While doing so, don't pay attention to what others think about your plans. Also set yourself free from past failures because to think outside the box, you have to think wide & deep.

Why are all these important?

Remember, YOU are always part of the communication and therefore the package. People may be interested in the offer per se? But if they are repulsed by the negotiator or the company? They simply will choose to go to someone else. It also shines in your sub communications, such as confidence and convictions.

You have to fight against your inner self to overcome feelings from past failures, otherwise you won't be able to anticipate future opportunities.

Try to separate your emotions (resentment, anger and worry) from the events.

Emotions are natural and human but once you are aware of them, you are able to gain control over them. Here acceptance is the key.

You may consider the following areas:

- What are you good at?
- Your positive traits that people you know have highlighted in the recent past?
- Your targeted goals in the coming 3 to 5 years?
- Things you want to avoid?
- Things you would like to pursue in your spare time in terms of volunteer work, spirituality, hobbies, career, learning etc.?
- Where would you like to see yourself from where you are today?
- Would you like your legacy to pass on to others such as your family members, community etc.?
- Are you sure you are ready to face challenges and make the commitment?

All answers to the above questions help in building your mission statement.

Making a commitment

In common language, commitment is a promise, a pledge or a binding obligation.

Commitment is always easier to take but quite difficult to follow through.

For instance, if you wish to have a lean body you have to change your eating habits. You actually have to commit to it!

Identifying your values

Values are the basic ethics, standards & principles in an individual's life.

It consists of your deeply held beliefs, attitude & behavior while communicating with others and vice versa.

In other words, values in the negotiation sense, are defined as your behavioral limits towards others and your expectations from them.

Planning ways to achieve your vision

After making your mission statement & knowing your values, you have to be clear about what you want and where are you planning to go.

To achieve your dreams, you have to set a clear path for yourself.

Renowned companies are clear while translating their vision into action such as McDonald's, as mentioned earlier.

Blockbuster was a rental movie store that didn't have an adult movie section which parents found it safe to send their kids to pick up movies there.

Similarly, many internet providers have incorporated predefined values into their businesses by inducing parental control blockers.

This has helped in gaining parents confidence that in their absence, their kids are not watching porn from questionable sites while surfing online.

The 3 year plan

The 3 year plan is one of the most important elements when planning for your personal and professional life.

It also consists of a backup plan, because it's possible that after a span of three years, you might fail to achieve 100% of whatever you have planned.

But if you are not clear about your vision for the next 3 more years, you will end up coasting in life, with no clear path. People who fail to achieve their goals do not bother to look ahead and develop a solid plan.

While developing your 3 year plans, consider the following factors in mind:

Think big- Don't pay attention to what has happened in the past. Be ambitious and think big!

Consider your future and move ahead.

Never get shattered by small thoughts.

Think bold- Consider your obstacles as a stepping stone to success.

Be creative when tackling all your problems in a unique way to get the best solutions on time.

Have a clear plan to convert your dreams into reality.

Think in sound bites- Think straight.

Do not include too many options while planning to avoid confusions because this may create hurdles and further confusions in succeeding your plans.

Maximizing gains must be your main aim behind the negotiations

Every organization works on its own ethical values but no organization works only to benefit its people irrespective of its goal i.e. profit making.

You must consider your organizational interest over the interest of anyone else.

However, you must not only consider your organizational interest above everything else. It means other people with whom you are dealing with must also be benefitted from you.

So being a negotiator, one must be able to create a win-win situation in every circumstance. Win-win negotiation is the best for all, because it creates a sense of satisfaction and goodwill in the mind of the other parties.

This paves the way for future deals too. A good deal is workable is most situations in real life. It is important on the part of the other parties that the deal is beneficial for them too.

A bad deal does not work in the long term, as it creates distrusts and burns bridges. It creates a lot of problems after the deal is finalized.

Below are some simple strategies that can help you create a win-win situation:

- No discount offer shall be made without getting a discount of the same kind or of a greater value.
- All negotiations beyond a fixed amount shall be matched with the already defined negotiation assets or the negotiation methodology.
- The purchasing, marketing or sales personnel conducting the negotiations shall be trained with the existing basic & advanced negotiation skills.

Dressing for success

Once you have prepared yourself for negotiation you have to dress for success. For example, your dressing style entirely depends upon the type of business you are into.

Similarly, if you are in the entertainment industry, your dressing style has to be appropriate for show business type people.

Folks working in animation studios are portrayed as dressed as if they are going to attend an afternoon barbeque.

Still, your dressing style varies as per your company's policies because even today, a lot of companies prefer the usual business attires in comparison to the more forward-looking, modern, informally dressed companies.

But it is always advisable to avoid dressing that is distracting or out of place for people you will be negotiating with.

While presenting your negotiation, you must consider the following points in mind:

- You must make sure that all the participants are present & listening to you carefully.
- State your reason for conducting the meeting.
- If you are using handouts, make sure that everyone has it with them and they are reading it carefully.
- Acknowledge everyone's feelings and attitudes while relating it to your purpose.
- Start your presentation as per the agenda, which is the very first step to start the negotiation process.

Mapping the opposition

One of the main reasons behind failure of negotiations is the lack of proper knowledge of the person with whom you are negotiating with.

Even if you are negotiating with more than one person, it is always advisable to remember at least the names of all of them.

A detailed knowledge about the other person helps you get into that person's mind as it were, and helps you gain insight to making the negotiation go your way.

It is imperative to put your energies towards such preparation.

Apart from the basic information about the negotiator, you must also discover few other helpful things such as:

- The negotiator's authority or power in this negotiation?

- His/ her client base?
- His interests?

You can also ask the above questions straightaway from the negotiator itself as these questions are the base of determining success in the negotiation.

Preparation plays a vital role, even if you know the person personally. Even when the person with whom you are negotiating is known to you, you must diligently prepare yourself for negotiation.

No successful negotiation can take place in the absence of proper preparation.

Gathering information

As discussed earlier, while gathering the information, the person with more knowledge, and knows how to leverage that information for persuasion purposes--wins the game.

It's a myth that power comes with clout, gruffness or size, but in fact the easiest and more reasonable way to build your power is through better preparation.

When you are prepared, you can win the world's toughest negotiation cases without too much effort.

One must have the urge and excitement while preparing.

The preparation process involves the following:

- Browsing the internet.
- Asking questions.
- Visiting the library.
- Consulting consumer reports.
- Reading insider reports.
- Asking around
- Profiling the negotiators of the other side, of how to push their buttons.

- Knowing your products, services or offers inside and out.

Setting a good goal

Setting your goals require disciplined focus and a lot of preparation.

The following things should be kept in mind while setting goals:

- You must have active participation from each and every member of your team.
- You must keep your goals on course.
- You must set the right goals.
- Your goals must be specific rather than general.
- Your goals must be attainable yet challenging.
- Don't sell yourself short.
- You must prioritize each of your goals.
- You must keep your long terms goals separate from your short term goals.

Setting the opening offer

An opening offer is the first specific statement that you set in a negotiation.

For instance, while appearing for a job interview, the opening offer could be that position and salary that you are looking for.

There are no magic formulas or hard and fast rules to determine the opening offer. The only way to determine it by focusing your goals and limits, while preparing for the negotiations.

It is important to note that your opening offer is always higher than your actual goals, but it should not be so high that you look unrealistic, inexperienced or foolish.

If you are a seller, then your opening offer is never lower than your actual goals and vice versa.

Setting & enforcing limits

Setting & enforcing limits is one of the most difficult lessons to learn during negotiation. Most people fail to enforce their limits while negotiating and over compromise just to close the deal. Setting limits help to save you a lot of time and effort from duds, as you are accepting only what is beneficial or acceptable to you.

In some situations, it also helps in rapid decision making.

As long as they do not go below the limits, further negotiation is possible, or just take the offer if you're in a hurry, and recoup your losses down the road.

As discussed earlier, also setting limits involve deep knowing that you have other choices too & detailed knowledge about what those choices are.

Components for a successful business negotiation

- Quality or acceptable deals or offers.
- Defining already set objectives for yourself and the other person.
- Considering and weighing down the various alternatives for the deal both for yourself and the other person.
- Using appropriate framing
- Creating a suitable negotiation climate
- Trade
- Close

How to convey your message to the other person when you have decided to walk away

On the basis of your honest judgment and solid preparation to end the negotiation in order to send a message and stop wasting each other's time. You must clearly state the circumstances under which the negotiation can be resumed back.

Be confident while walking away and avoid any kind of hesitation while saying the last parting words.

If you are in an angry mood, avoid terminating the negotiation in that moment.

Cool your head and think about it first before making hasty decisions you might regret later on. Instead, take a break before terminating the negotiation as it also helps to avoid damaging your reputation and coming off unprofessional.

The role of listening in the negotiation process

Not only in negotiations, but listening is the basis for all types of interpersonal activities. Good listening skills can help you achieve huge success by changing your personal and professional results, because you understand people and situations much more in-depth, and you are better at navigating them.

It is often seen that women who divorce their spouse often give reasons that the husband's do not listen to them.

Similarly, people do not buy goods from those vendors who do not listen carefully to their requirements.

Research has shown that people who are not listened to carefully feel unloved, ignored and unimportant.

In other words, listening is fully soaking in the entire information communicated by the other party.

This gives comfort to the other person that somebody is truly listening to him.

The two best ways for better listening is restating (repeat the words) and paraphrasing (recounting the information in your own words.)

There are basically 6 barriers that restrict you from being a good listener:

- Weak self-confidence.
- Your defensive behavior (seen in your eyes, hands, body, feet, and tone of voice).
- Your energy drag and patience level.
- Your habits (in terms of thinking of something else when the other person is talking to you).
- Preconception.
- Your belief of not expecting value in others

Becoming a good listener can help you in various other ways.

Make a habit of taking notes while the other person is communicating with you, so that you do not end up forgetting something important that was conveyed to you.

Build a habit of asking questions when things are not clear to you. Don't feel shy while doing this.

When you think that your energies are becoming low, sit straight, lean forward, make eye contact, uncross your legs and arms so that you can keep yourself awake all the time.

Drink coffee or tea or even energy drinks if you think it will help.

Strategies to succeed with difficult customers during negotiation

- Patient listening
- Show empathy
- Slow down speech and lower the voice
- Imagine a good or receptive audience (positivity)

- It's good to be wrong to make the other person right
- Know that it's not personal
- Demonstrate emotional control

Asking the right questions

Asking questions is good during negotiation but you must take care that the questions asked relate to the negotiation or open doors to knowledge about the other person.

To get positive results, effective questioning at the time of negotiating is extremely important. Hence, a person involved in the negotiation process must develop the ability to ask quality questions, that will help him get what he wants!

At the same time, these questions must not be confrontational & bombastic, but must be easy to understand and aims to extract specific information.

Battling the Jargon

Don't feel embarrassed or shy while asking questions for the purpose of extending your knowledge.

In long conversations, people often use shorthand or jargon while talking and it is important for you to know the proper meaning of such words.

For example, when a marketing head talks about AMC it means American Multi-Cinema. Those who are not familiar with this term may understand it as Advanced Marketing Chapter. Both these terms hold different meanings and are used in different contexts. So when a person is confused it is always wise to clarify. Situations may arise that a person using such a term may be from the same industry as you & will expect you to know the meaning of the terms used.

To ask questions about the meaning of such words, may make you feel embarrassed. But don't feel shy while asking and just go ahead and put an end to your curiosity. At the same time, it is also important to clarify confusing words.

Relative words are descriptive and nonspecific words that hold meaning only in relation to something else.

Some of these words are substantial, soon, many large, high quality, cheap etc. Never feel shy while asking for clarification when such words are used.

For instance, if a customer comes up to you and says that he is looking ahead to place an "big order" from you.

In such situation you should never feel shy clarifying the meaning of "big order".

You may say something like this; Sir, by "big order" do you mean to place orders in thousands, hundreds or tens? At the same time, it is always advisable to note down the information so that you do not forget about your customer's future plans.

Asking questions is your real power.

Guidelines to ask quality questions

- Plan your questions in advance.
- Your questions must have a purpose.
- Tailor your questions as per your listener's interest.
- Purge general questions with more precise ones.
- Keep your questions simple, clear and short covering only one subject at a time.
- Make adjustments with your questions and their answers.
- Avoid interrupting, while the other person is talking to you.

Hence effective questioning leads to deep understanding, rapport establishment, better listening, better follow up and higher motivation.

Role of body language while listening

All of us recognize emotions such as love, hatred, happiness, sadness and fear even in unspoken communication from others.

Research has shown that 90% of our communication is non-verbal.

Thus, your ability to understand and use your body language is one of the best ways to improve your negotiating and communication skills and in sizing up the other party.

If you lack fluency in your body communications, it is advisable to practice it regularly.

This can help you recognize nervousness, boredom, resistance which can further help you become a smart and more effective negotiator.

Different attitudes are associated with different non-verbal communications.

Being a negotiator, you have to perform two main tasks:

First, your body language must be able to clearly convey the messages you intend to convey.

Second, excellent reading abilities of the non-verbal signals produced by the other person.

Looking at the person's gestures, you must be able to identify conflicting actions and words.

Likewise identify points of interest.

Do their eyes light up when you bring up a particular subject?

Perhaps this information can be used to strengthen your negotiation position.

It is extremely important for you to match your body language with your words. If you fail to do so, you must find out reasons for the same.

Some of these reasons may be:

- Energy drain or burnout.
- Lack of concentration while communicating.
- Development of bad communication habits.

Tune in with your inner voice

Your subconscious mind or your inner voice is always active and talking to you. Your inner voice guides you to be ethical and honest but still many people choose to ignore it.

Studies have revealed that women will more often listen to their intuition or inner voices in comparison with men and thus make wiser decisions in life.

To bring out your inner voice, you must practice quieting your mind and other brain techniques.

Being crystal clear by expressing your views

None of us are born to express clear ideas nor there is a specific way that will determine the way you should express your ideas to people.

However, there are several ways in which you can conduct yourself, write, and speak, at the different stages of negotiation.

Being crystal clear does not mean that you are revealing your position straight away. It just means that whenever you speak, write or communicate to the person in front of you, you must be able to communicate your intentions and messages effectively and clearly.

Organizing your thoughts

Before trying to organize your thoughts, you must be clear about your listener's needs and wants as well.

You must also try to access the experience of the other person. This can help you judge the background or what makes the other person tick.

Once you know this, you can find out how much attention or emphasis should be on the different aspects of your presentation.

The last step is to organize your thoughts clearly which can be done depending upon your type of presentation.

Few tips and tricks for being clear:

- Describing the steps involved while pursuing the tasks.
- Set the climate.
- Cite available resources.
- Paint the big picture.
- Invite questions.
- Summarizing the other person's strategy or input.
- Agree on a follow up date.

Keep your commitments

Clarity is also determined by the consistency in your speech and execution of your ideas. Keeping your commitments during negotiation is a very important part.

For instance, a lazy employee comes up to you, looking into your eyes and promises that he will finish his task by 3:00 PM.

If by 3:00 PM he completes the work as promised, then he succeeds in gaining your trust. While if the same employee comes up to you, gives the same promise and fails? He will squander away the trust that you had in him.

So if you are making any kind of commitment with the other person, make sure you do it and on time!

Breaking your commitment can spoil your image and can make the other party confused and upset. Such kinds of behavior on your part is considered as unprofessional and as such will spread through word of mouth with other people working with you.

Write it down

Writing helps you make your commitments clearer and precise because when ideas are encapsulated in words, they get solidified with proper meaning and purpose.

Writing your thoughts may help you objectify and handle problem areas too.

Some tips for writing clear communication includes the following:

- Use short but precise wording.
- Stick only to one major idea while writing each paragraph.
- Use simpler words when possible.
- Write in such a manner that your writing clearly separates the beginning, middle & end of your communication.
- Complete your sentences.
- Avoid the use of abbreviations and jargon unless the person in front of you uses them often. This should be avoided even when you are writing to the person working in the same profession as you. However, abbreviations become necessary or acceptable as shorthand only if it's been clearly established the beginning of the communication.
- Don't abbreviate to new people. They might not know them yet.
- Be precise while writing. Note: No matter how long your written communication is, you should not be afraid to cover important facts and figures that you think should not be missed.

Encouraging others to clarify

People often feel humiliated when others tell them that they are a bad communicators or have difficulties comprehending, which is akin to calling them stupid.

When someone lacks or need help in their communications, your duty is to pull that person up to speed. You have to be tactful while doing this because the person will open up only when he/ she feels comfortable.

Your way to tackle the person depends upon the type of person you are dealing with, and your personal style.

Capturing the audience

Clarity helps in making a good presentation. It can help you succeed in this regard on your next negotiation:

- Set your goals & keep it handy.
- Analyze your audience.
- Be confident as confidence is the key to success in convincing them you know what you're talking about.
- Do your homework and create the talking points that will push their buttons in the best way possible.
- Manage expectations, don't over hype or under deliver while overpromising
- Plan your presentation step-by-step. Plan the format of your presentation in advance.

Barriers to clarity

Clarity is always accompanied by a few barriers. The biggest of all is lack of concentration. In order to succeed, you must first learn to identify these barriers and must take appropriate actions to eradicate them.

Other such barriers are:

- Fear of rejection.
- Fear of hurting someone's feelings.

- General distractions such as laziness, fatigue etc.

Note: If you fail to maintain clarity of the audience by fully understanding your communication techniques, you must be prepared to pay the price.

Even when you have given your 100%, you may end up losing the deal when you fail to keep things very clear. The absence of clarity makes your offer full of holes and unrealistic

Turn off the anger buttons by pushing the pause buttons

At stressful situations, it is advisable to push your pause button.

This can be done anywhere, say a home, office, wherever you need a little space. In simple words, turning off the hot buttons keeps your negotiation stable and allows you to sort out your problems later on.

In this time frame, you can review your conversation so that if you are missing anything, you can update it later on.

Individuals use their pause button when things get heated or there is an impasse.

Your success in winning the negotiation depends on how smartly you play your cards, including using the pause button.

No matter how hard the situation becomes, your pause button will give you space to calm down and move ahead.

However, the pause button is accompanied by various factors, as:

Not knowing when to pause.

Learn to pause before you are about to concede. It allows you to think things carefully.

When you pause under pressure, it aids you in giving into these pressures.

Using the pause button takes a good amount of understanding and observation. This is because when the person sitting in front of you is also trying the same tactics of using the pause button to win the negotiation? You must avoid using the pause button in that way because the other person will be on to you.

And if you are aware that the other person is about to use the pause button?

Be explicit about your wants and then take the break.

Synchronize between your hot button & other emotional responses

Human beings are full of emotions & responses

Therefore, your involvement in a negotiation doesn't keep you away from your emotions.

For instance, if you request your coworker to do something on your behalf in your absence & you get a blunt response "that's not my job"? In such a situation, you may lash out at her by saying "that's not mine either".

Such situations do not give you enough time to turn off your hot button and act wisely. So it is always advisable to exercise better control over your emotions.

Each one of us have different hot buttons.

You have to identify them and learn to deal with them in times of need.

Your attitude plays a big role during a negotiation

You must always carry a positive attitude even when you think that deal is falling through, because you never know what's in store for you ahead.

Just like crying, yawning & laughing is infectious, same is the case with attitude.

- Shake hands to communicate you're a good sport and that things are okay.
- Reflect and share your thoughts to your counterparts which can help you send a signal of openness.

Tips to maintain a positive attitude during negotiation:

- Look for the good in the negotiation and the negotiators.

- Look for the lessons you can learn from this interaction, and possibly improve upon with the next client.
- Keep your focus on the solution not the problem.
- Avoid focusing on the unhelpful past and direct it forward and how you can positively affect the future.

Thomas Jefferson has rightly said "Nothing can stop the man with the right mental attitude from achieving his goal; nothing on earth can help the man with the wrong mental attitude".

Dealing with discouragement

Even after putting so much hard work to close the deal (say selling) it may be accompanied with a lot of failures and rejections, until you get to that place where you get exactly what you want.

This may result in discouragement and frustration at first.

In such situations, you must learn to be calm and look ahead for future opportunities to explore.

Those individuals who know well to turn failures into opportunities have higher success ratios than failure. This is because failures are the stepping stone to success.

You learn with every mistake! As the saying goes, "Sometimes you win, sometimes you learn." This particular deal may fall through, but at least you get to polish your techniques, which will help you on the next one.

Tips to convert failure into opportunity:
- Try taking different views of the situation that can yield results.
- Think outside the box, explore it from a different angles et cetera.
- Once you have failed here, keep your mind fresh and positive before entering into the next negotiation.

- Take some time off if necessary to regain composure and motivation.
- You need a positive mindset and confidence to amp up your success rates. This is not optional.
- Keep all the negative thoughts away and try to learn from the situation. Actually put down to paper what went wrong, so you can systematically correct each one, for the next client. Try finding out reasons behind your failures with a positive attitude.
- You have to fight with your inner self to overcome failures, otherwise you won't be able to look ahead for future opportunities.
- Try to separate your emotions (resentment, anger, disappointment and worry) from the events. Emotions are natural and human but once you are aware of them you can gain control over them. Here, acceptance is the key.

Dealing with difficult situations and people

In this instance, the main resentment at the time of failure is not because your negotiation has failed per se. It is because of the way the other person has behaved inappropriately.

Some people are so selfish, one-sided and in the habit of putting themselves and their wants irrationally above others. Although there is nothing wrong with that and is encouraged to an extent? You still have to respect the fact that other people have their own needs and wants to satisfy as well.

Some of these people go to any extent just to get what they want unethically.

While doing so, they don't mind hurting others.

If negotiation is a part of your daily professional life, you must possess the know-how on the art of dealing with such people. Never get into resentment and anger.

Be professional!

Tips that can help you deal with such situations:

- Try to validate instead of resisting the person's hurtful remarks.
- Acknowledge the truth.
- Assess your situation.
- Take concrete action.
- Guard your reputation at any cost.
- Avoid sinking into the other person's level.
- Don't allow the problem to fester other areas.
- Make the first move to remedy the situation, even if it means getting out of the negotiation yourself.
- Keep it private.
- Be realistic while applying the above tactics.

None of these tricks are easy but still can help you show people that you are not a victim.

Things that can help you enhance your negotiation outcomes

There are certain things that should be immediately implemented to have a significant impact in enhancing your negotiation results.

However, you must apply it in the right manner to gain positive results.

Define your negotiation strategies in advance. You should have different approaches, for different situations, different types of clients, and the different products and services you may be offering.

There is no one size fits all approach. Learn to customize your approach to maximize your chances of success.

There must be clarity about those individuals and groups who are most suited to negotiate wisely for you in this particular instance. For example, if you are selling medical and computer products? You would want the medical specialist team to handle that particular negotiation.

Highlight the characteristics or strengths and weaknesses of the different negotiators in your organization. Assign the best people who will get the job done.

Define and measure success in the negotiation environment. Success can mean different things. You have to define what success and failure conditions are.

Choose the best particular actions, strategies and tactics suitable in implementing your negotiation strategy.

Taking stock of the indicators of how you measure success at the time of negotiations? In other words, tracking of the metrics or specific variables in a particular negotiation offer.

Are you ready to give discounts, as a gesture of goodwill to the other person even when you do not get any type of concession of equal or greater value? Are you prepared to offer some of your products and services to your clients free of cost, in order to win some deals in the future? For example, it's not uncommon to initially offer your services especially for those firms that are still trying to build their credibility and reputation. By initially offering free services, they absorb the risk and get free word-of-mouth advertising if they do a good job, or their services are exemplary.

Closing the deal- The glory moment

The closing comes with a lot of hardships and anticipation for both parties.

It is a reward in return for all your hard work that was done before the end part is reached.

But closing should not be considered as the only satisfactory resolution of a negotiation.

Closing the deal should come with smooth performance throughout the life of your agreement.

In other words, you have to deliver exactly what you promised or else risk tarnishing your credibility and possibly losing future deals from that client and others.

Your deal must be closed only when it has become a good deal or a win-win for all the parties involved.

Usually people accept all the terms just to close the deal quickly. This should not be done because all the promises must be met as agreed upon.

There are various factors that a person has to keep in mind while closing the deal.

Even when you realize that the chances to close the deal are minimum, there should be no room for fake commitments.

A deal is closed in 3 ways:

- Win-win negotiation
- Exceptional deals
- Better deal than the one they had.

I excluded zero-sum, or win-lose negotiations as it is not a sustainable way to conduct business. However, that is still one of the possible outcomes. Win-win negotiation is the best of all because it creates a sense of satisfaction in the mind of everyone concerned, and paves the way for future deals.

A good deal is workable under most circumstances but not all.

A bad one one-sided deal does not work in the long run as I've mentioned. Instead it creates a lot of problems after the deal is finalized. It is more trouble than its worth.

Assessing the deal

Assessment of the particulars of any deal is necessary before closing it.

Some points may have been misunderstood and need clarifications or adjustments on the terms may have to be made. Make sure that the deal you are planning to close is actually a good deal for you in the long haul. Can you actually fulfill on your promises?

Consider the following questions in mind before you proceed:

Get into the details of not only the actual deal but the other person and find out why he/ she is interested in dealing with you?

The offer may be sound, but there might be conflicts of interest elsewhere, or how they conduct business etc.

- Analyze whether the other person is indeed capable to take on the agreement and fulfil the contract as agreed upon?
- Does the agreement relate to your future goals & does the result fits into your mission/vision statement?
- Would associating yourself with this company help your reputation or tarnish it?
- Does the agreement fit into the original objectives you set out to get from this negotiation?
- Or along the way, did you make too many concessions and alterations in the deal? Before proceeding further, make sure everything is in order.
- Are the people involved in the negotiation ready to take the responsibility to carry the agreement forward despite unforeseeable events and are the ready to do what it takes to fulfil the deal?
- Do they have the infrastructure in case something goes wrong?

If the answers to all the above questions are yes, then you must go ahead to finalize the deal. But if you are not sure about the answer to any of these questions, then you must invest some more time to do so extra research, explore other options & push your pause button momentarily, in order to fix it.

If possible, try to make changes to convert all the doubtful or iffy answers to solid yeses.

Once all the answers are converted to yes, just move ahead and close the deal right away.

After all the above things are done, don't backtrack.

This is because this may annoy the person sitting in front of you when you continue on poking holes in finding additional flaws, when the process has already been done and fixed. Don't go overboard with this.

Highlighting new points when everything is going smoothly doesn't make any sense, and you might come off as trying to take advantage, by trying to get more.

No one likes to deal with a person who ends up wasting time just for the sake of some additional advantage instead of closing the deal they should already have closed and moving on!

Close the deal so that the deal doesn't go out of your hand.

Win-win deals

Some negotiations are very clear, as both the parties are quite straightforward about their interests and absolute limits. Both meet each other's criteria for success.

Psychological barriers to closing

- Fear of rejection.
- Fear of failure.
- Fear of making mistakes.
- Fear of criticism.
- Fear of commitment.
- Fear of loss.
- Fear of getting underhanded and being taken advantage of

The hurdles while closing the deal may just be cold feet and not due to you or any other external factors. Here you have to fight your own demons and go ahead with the deal.

Once you have identified your fears and other blocks, take steps to eradicate them or at least work around them.

Once the deal is done and the legal contracts are signed, follow the last step.

Grab a few drinks and celebrate!

The authors, publishers, and distributors of this guide have made every effort to ensure the validity, accuracy, and timely nature of the information presented here However, no guarantee is made, neither direct nor implied, that the information in this guide or the techniques described herein are suitable for or applicable to any given individual person or group of persons, nor that any specific result will be achieved The authors, publishers, and distributors of this guide will be held harmless and without fault in all situations and causes arising from the use of this information by any person, with or without professional medical supervision The information contained in this book is for informational and entertainment purposes only It not intended as a professional advice or a recommendation to act

No part of this book may be reproduced or transmitted in any form whatsoever, electronic, or mechanical, including photocopying, recording, or by any informational storage or retrieval system without express permission from the author

© Copyright 2018, JNR Publishing

All rights reserved

Other books by the author

The Complete Day Trading Education for Beginners: a course book to successfully setup & learn the rules, secrets, techniques, psychology, systems & strategy for stocks, futures, forex, etfs & more

Mastering Business Social Media Marketing Theory & Practice: book covers the fundamental facts & strategies, automation & advanced ideas & tips on corporate social marketing for businesses & beyond

Investing In Stock Market For Beginners: Understanding the basics of how to make money with stocks

Real Ways to Make Money Fast Online from Home for Beginners: quickly make easy money on the internet for kids, teens stay at home moms, freelance writers, college students & more...

The Best Real Estate Book for Beginners: Winning in the game of Real Estate Investments!

Customer Service Care Support Success for Life: Exceptional client services, support & behavior by becoming customer centric & obsessed to improve retention, engagement, experience & lifetime value

Made in the USA
Coppell, TX
28 December 2023